AVERAGE
DAY IN
JAPAN...

ON AN AVERAGE DAY IN JAPAN...

TOM HEYMANN

FAWCETT COLUMBINE • NEW YORK

A Fawcett Columbine Book
Published by Ballantine Books

Library of Congress Catalog Card Number: 92-90066
ISBN: 0-449-90607-8

Cover design by Dale Fiorillo

Manufactured in the United States of America

First Edition: September 1992

10 9 8 7 6 5 4 3 2 1

To my family,
for their continued
love and support.

ACKNOWLEDGMENTS

I want to thank my friends, and literary agents, Herbert and Nancy Katz, for their encouragement and sense of humor. Also, to my editor, Elisa Wares, for her guidance and support.

AUTHOR'S NOTE

In compiling this book, every effort has been made to ensure that the information included is reliable and represents the most current state of affairs. Author's notes have been added to most entries to provide additional insights, whether through a comparison with the United States or by further explanation. Notes do not appear if that entry is self-explanatory or no relevant comparative information could be found.

All Japanese monetary values have been translated into dollars (from yen) at the rate of 130 yen = $1.

INTRODUCTION

Modern Japanese–American relations can best be described as intense, if not strained. From the Japanese bombing of Pearl Harbor during World War II (and the U.S. atomic response), to the automobile trade wars of the 1980s, Japan has been the country Americans love to hate.

Japan is a country comprised of four major islands (and 3,900 smaller ones). While the country's land mass only approaches that of California, Japan's population stands at a considerable 122,783,000 (and growing at the rate of 1,422 persons each day) or approximately one-half that of the United States. In addition to allowing for some easy comparisons with the U.S. (simply multiply the Japanese statistic by two), Japan's population makes for a very crowded country. There are currently 200 Japanese for every square mile of land while in the U.S. just 16 Americans vie for every square mile.

Once upon a time in the world, the Japanese measured themselves against America. The "Made in Japan" insignia was a certain indication that the product would not last very long. Consumers longed to acquire American, and European, goods. Today, the tables have turned and Americans (and most of the world) view Japan as the standard-bearer in many aspects of business, finance, technology, and health.

What has happened to bring about this dramatic shift? Clearly it is more than just a 6-day school week and a workday that regularly extends well into the night six or seven days each week, that have caused the Japanese to assume a position of world dominance. Analysts have noted that the Japanese possess a hunger for success, likely the same kind of hunger that drove the United States to world dominance through much of its relatively short history.

On an Average Day in Japan . . . explores these and other pertinent issues. In an effort to provide a statistical portrait of today's Japan, *On an Average Day in Japan* . . . takes the reader through one day in the land of the rising yen.

ON AN AVERAGE DAY IN
AVERAGE
DAY IN
JAPAN...

ON AN AVERAGE DAY...

... 3,600 new Japanese are born

... 2,173 Japanese die

NOTE: In the United States, 10,501 new Americans are born and
5,937 Americans die.

# ON AN AVERAGE DAY...

... the number of new babies born
  decreases by 89

NOTE: The shrinking birthrate is causing great concern in Japan.
  Partly to blame are the increasing number of women in the
  workforce and a tendency toward later marriages. In the
  United States, the number of births increases daily by 216.

4

ON AN AVERAGE DAY...

Of the 3,600 babies who are born,

... 52 are delivered by midwives, friends, or family members

NOTE: In the United States, 384 of the 10,501 new babies are delivered by midwives, friends, or family members.

5

ON AN AVERAGE DAY...

... 23 sets of twins are born

NOTE: In the United States, 217 sets of twins are born.

ON AN AVERAGE DAY...

... 336,392 Japanese celebrate birthdays

NOTE: 673,693 Americans celebrate birthdays.

⛩ON AN AVERAGE DAY...

... 5,041 Japanese become teenagers

... 5,420 Japanese turn 18

... 6,578 Japanese turn 40

NOTE: The United States is also a rapidly aging society. On an average day, 8,838 Americans become teenagers, 9,951 turn 18, and 10,951 turn 40.

ON AN AVERAGE DAY...

... the population grows by 1,422 persons

Of these,

... 715 are males

... 707 are females

NOTE: In the United States, the population grows by 6,315 persons. Of these, 3,195 are males and 3,120 are females.

9

♟ON AN AVERAGE DAY...

... 1,940 Japanese couples are married
... 422 Japanese couples are divorced

NOTE: In the United States, 6,567 couples are married and 3,197 couples are divorced. In both countries, the marriage and divorce rates have been declining in recent years.

ON AN AVERAGE DAY...

... 534 "arranged" marriages take place

... 1,406 "love" marriages take place

NOTE: While on the decline in Japan, arranged marriages still comprise more than 1 in 3 of today's weddings.

ON AN AVERAGE DAY...

... 475 children find themselves in one-
parent families because of divorce

NOTE: In the United States, 2,989 children find themselves in one-
parent families because of divorce.

ON AN AVERAGE DAY...

... the number of single-member
households grows by 433

13

ON AN AVERAGE DAY...

... 30 women forty years of age or older
give birth to new babies

NOTE: The number of later pregnancies is on the rise in both the
United States and Japan. At least partly responsible for this
change is a trend toward later marriages and the growing
number of women in the workforce. On an average day in
the United States, 99 women forty years of age or older give
birth to new babies.

ON AN AVERAGE DAY...

... 1,279 women receive abortions

NOTE: With oral contraception still illegal in Japan, abortion continues to be one of the country's leading forms of birth control. In the United States, 3,477 abortions are performed.

ON AN AVERAGE DAY...

... 124 young women under the age of twenty became pregnant

Of those,

... 77 receive abortions

... 47 give birth to babies

NOTE: In the United States, 2,064 young women under the age of twenty become pregnant. Of those, 769 receive abortions and 1,295 give birth to babies.

ON AN AVERAGE DAY...

... 6 cases of child abuse are reported

NOTE: It is widely believed that the number of child-abuse cases in Japan is underreported. In contrast to reporting procedures in the United States, Japanese who report cases of child abuse are responsible for substantiating their claims. In the United States, 5,753 cases of child abuse are reported every day.

ON AN AVERAGE DAY...

... 287 children run away from home

Of those,

... 148 are boys

... 139 are girls

NOTE: In the United States, 2,740 children run away from home. Of those, 514 become involved in crimes. Of Japan's 287 runaways, 6 become involved in crimes.

ON AN AVERAGE DAY...

... 32 children under the age of fifteen
  die

  Of those,

... 17 die before reaching their first
  birthday

NOTE: In the United States, 151 children under the age of fifteen
die. Of those, 119 die before reaching their first birthday.

ON AN AVERAGE DAY...

... 10 children die from birth-related defects

NOTE: In the United States, 122 children die from birth-related defects.

ON AN AVERAGE DAY...

... 563 Japanese die of cancer

... 433 Japanese die of heart disease

... 353 Japanese die of strokes

... 156 Japanese die of pneumonia

... 83 Japanese die in accidents

... 67 Japanese die in suicides

... 47 Japanese die from chronic liver disease and cirrhosis

NOTE: A diet low in fat has long been credited for Japan's low incidence of heart disease. In the United States, the leading causes of death include: heart disease (2,113); cancer (1,265); strokes (419); accidents (256); pneumonia (185); diabetes (101); suicide (81) and chronic liver disease and cirrhosis (73).

ON AN AVERAGE DAY...

Of the 83 Japanese who die in accidents,

... 37 die in motor-vehicle accidents

... 11 die in falls

... 8 die from drowning

... 6 die in fires

NOTE: As in Japan, the leading causes of accidental deaths in the United States are motor-vehicle accidents, falls, drowning, and fires.

ON AN AVERAGE DAY...

... 4 Japanese die in motorcycle
accidents

NOTE: 10 Americans die in motorcycle accidents.

ON AN AVERAGE DAY...

... 8 Japanese drown

Of those,

... 1 is a child under the age of fifteen

NOTE: In the United States, 14 Americans drown. Of those, 4 are children under the age of fifteen.

24

ON AN AVERAGE DAY...

... 67 Japanese commit suicide

   Of those,

... 43 are men

... 24 are women

NOTE: In the United States, 84 Americans commit suicide. Of those, 67 are men and 17 are women.

ON AN AVERAGE DAY...

... 2 people under the age of twenty
commit suicide

NOTE: In the United States, 7 people under the age of twenty
commit suicide.

ON AN AVERAGE DAY...

... 80 Japanese die of lung cancer

Of those,

... 58 are men

... 22 are women

NOTE: In the United States, 332 Americans die of lung cancer. Of those, 233 are men and 99 are women.

ON AN AVERAGE DAY...

... 1,289 Japanese receive treatment for medical conditions that resulted from U.S. atomic bombs dropped on Hiroshima and Nagasaki during World War II

NOTE: More than 350,000 atomic bomb victims are still living. Each year, the Japanese government spends nearly $1 billion treating these sufferers.

ON AN AVERAGE DAY...

... 11,210 Japanese are on waiting lists
for kidney transplants

Of those,

... 2 receive transplants

NOTE: 17,940 Americans are on waiting lists for kidney transplants.
Of those, 25 receive transplants. In contrast to the situation
in the United States, very few organs in Japan are obtained
from anonymous donors.

♣ON AN AVERAGE DAY...

... the average Japanese requires an average of $2.84 in healthcare

Of that, an average of

... $1.55 is paid by insurance

... $.95 is paid by the government

... $.34 is paid by the patient

NOTE: The average American faces an average of $6.45 in healthcare expenses each day. Of that, $2.55 is paid by government, $2.05 is paid by private insurance, and $1.85 is paid by the patient. Not only is the cost of healthcare in the U.S. the highest in the world, but Americans are forced to pay more than twice as much of their medical costs as the Japanese.

ON AN AVERAGE DAY...

... 121,555,170 Japanese are covered by
at least one health insurance policy

NOTE: An estimated 37 million Americans are not covered by any
health insurance policy. It is a source of pride in Japan that
fully 99 percent of their people are covered by health
insurance.

ON AN AVERAGE DAY...

... 215,856 Japanese are living in nursing homes

NOTE: More than 1.3 million Americans reside in nursing homes. In addition to a strong societal sense of family, the Japanese government has made a concerted effort to make it easier for its elderly citizens to continue living at home.

ON AN AVERAGE DAY...

... 1,405,000 Japanese over the age of sixty-five are living alone

... 8,345,000 are living with their children

NOTE: In the United States, 8,664,000 Americans over the age of sixty-five live alone. In stark contrast to Japan, American culture has not maintained a sense of familial responsibility for its older citizens.

ON AN AVERAGE DAY...

... approximately 2,200,000 Japanese are
alcoholics

NOTE: There are approximately 10,500,000 alcoholics in the United
States.

🏯ON AN AVERAGE DAY...

... 923 Japanese are arrested for
drunken driving

NOTE: 4,932 Americans are arrested for driving under the influence
of alcohol.

ON AN AVERAGE DAY...

... 14,178,747 Japanese are overweight
   Of those,
... 5,833,728 are men
... 8,345,019 are women

NOTE: A much larger percentage of Americans is overweight. In total, 46,000,096 Americans fit into this category. Of those, 21,310,405 are men and 24,689,691 are women.

ON AN AVERAGE DAY...

... 33,474,710 Japanese smoke

Of those,

... 27,345,600 are men

... 6,129,110 are women

NOTE: While a smaller percentage of American men smoke
(33 percent versus 63 percent in Japan), a much larger
percentage of American women light up (28 percent versus
13 percent in Japan). In total, 54,847,517 American adults
smoke. Of those, 28,946,634 are men and 25,900,883 are
women. Smoking is losing its allure among Japanese men
(from a shocking 84 percent in 1966), while it remains
steady with Japanese women.

ON AN AVERAGE DAY...

... 8,337,188 Japanese children under
   the age of eighteen smoke

NOTE: In the United States, approximately 3 million children smoke
      cigarettes on a daily basis. These child smokers consume
      nearly 1 billion packs of cigarettes each year. The problem of
      child smoking, though, is much more prevalent in Japan. In
      response to a surge in smoking among the young, tobacco
      advertising is being subjected to increasing government
      regulation.

ON AN AVERAGE DAY...

... Japanese smoke 849,315,069
    cigarettes

    Of those,

... 195,342,466 are "Mild Sevens"

NOTE: Americans smoke 1,437,315,068 cigarettes each day. Of those, 380,888,493 are "Marlboros." Though rarely seen outside of Japan, Japan Tobacco Inc.'s "Mild Seven" is the world's second best selling brand, after Philip Morris' "Marlboro."

⛩ON AN AVERAGE DAY...

... the number of cigarettes smoked
increases by 19,178,082

NOTE: An antismoking movement has yet to make its presence felt
in Japan. Meanwhile, cigarette consumption in the United
States falls by 90,876,712 cigarettes each day.

ON AN AVERAGE DAY...

... 163 fires are reported

In which,

... 6 Japanese are killed

... 21 Japanese are injured

NOTE: In the United States, 6,384 fires are reported in which 16 Americans are killed and 77 are injured.

ON AN AVERAGE DAY...

Of Japan's 163 fires,

... 24 are started by arson

NOTE: Of America's 6,384 daily fires, 222 are caused by arson.

ON AN AVERAGE DAY...

... fires cause $3,035,216 in damages

NOTE: In the United States, fires cause $19,693,151 in damages.

ON AN AVERAGE DAY...

... 7 acres are burned by forest fires

NOTE: On an average day in the United States, 5,951 acres are burned by forest fires.

ON AN AVERAGE DAY...

... 11,766,667 acres of land are used for growing crops

Of that land,

... 7,413,000 acres are irrigated

NOTE: Irrigation has become a critical part of the world's efforts to feed its growing population. In Japan, where people are many and land is scarce, irrigation is currently employed on 63 percent of the cropland. In the United States, where less crowded conditions prevail, just 10 percent of the nation's 469,490,000 acres of cropland receive irrigation.

ON AN AVERAGE DAY...

... the amount of Japanese farmland
decreases by 257 acres

NOTE: The amount of American farmland decreases by 10,959 acres
daily. At the same time, the average American farm has
grown from 426 acres in 1980 to 456 acres today. Japan has
similarly experienced a trend toward larger farms.

ON AN AVERAGE DAY...

... 147 acres of farmland are converted to other uses

Of those,

... 49 acres are converted to housing

... 43 acres are used for construction

... 30 acres are used for mining

... 22 acres are converted to forest lands

NOTE: Most of America's "lost" farmland is converted to one or another industrial use.

ON AN AVERAGE DAY...

...the amount of forest land grows by
166 acres

NOTE: Surveys show that parts of Europe and Japan are the only
areas increasing their forest lands. In the United States, the
amount of forested land decreases by 1,644 acres.

ON AN AVERAGE DAY...

... the number of bicycles in use increases by 4,060

NOTE: With more than 60 million bicycles, the Japanese have twice as many bikes as they do cars. The United States, in contrast, has 103 million bikes and more than 140 million cars.

ON AN AVERAGE DAY...

... the number of cars in use increases
by 3,153

ON AN AVERAGE DAY...

... 9,405,000 Japanese workers use
bicycles to commute to work or to
commuter rail stations

NOTE: Fewer than 1 million American workers use bicycles to make
their way to work.

ON AN AVERAGE DAY...

... nearly 50,000,000 Japanese workers use public transportation to get to and from work

NOTE: Fewer than 10 million American workers use public transportation to get to and from work each day. In fact, the number of Americans using public transportation for commutation has been on a steady decline.

ON AN AVERAGE DAY...

... 10,726,027 Japanese travel by subway
   Of those,
... 6,704,110 travel on the Tokyo subway
   system

NOTE: The Japanese rely to a much greater extent on mass
transportation. On an average day in the U.S. 6,323,288
Americans travel by subway. Of those, 3,700,000 ride the New
York City subway system.

ON AN AVERAGE DAY...

...the price of riding a Tokyo subway is
$.78

NOTE: The price of riding the New York City subway is $1.25.

ON AN AVERAGE DAY...

... 687,671 tons of carbon are emitted into the air

... the amount of carbon emitted into the air increases by 18,975 tons

NOTE: Carbon is produced by the burning of fossil fuels and forest fires. Each ton of carbon emitted into the air causes 3.7 tons of carbon dioxide to be produced, accounting for about half of the global warming occurring today. The United States is the world's largest contributor of carbon, releasing 3,353,425 tons of the substance each day. This number is currently increasing at the daily rate of 410,959 tons.

ON AN AVERAGE DAY...

... motorists dump 147,945 pounds of garbage at highway rest stops

... the amount of garbage dumped increases by 12,524 pounds

NOTE: The dramatic increase in highway garbage is attributed to an increase in the number of disposable products, and the growing number of vending machines in Japan.

🏯 ON AN AVERAGE DAY...

... 3,618,000 pounds of medical waste is generated

Including

... 708,000 pounds that are hazardous

NOTE: Like the U.S., Japan has been finding some of its infectious medical waste mixed in with the regular trash. In the United States, 17,534,000 pounds of medical waste is generated including 2,191,781 pounds that are infectious.

ON AN AVERAGE DAY...

... 240,000,000 pounds of trash is
produced (2 pounds per person)
Of that,
... 96,000,000 pounds are recycled

NOTE: A scarcity of vacant land has forced the Japanese to be more
vigilant in their efforts to recycle. The Japanese now recycle
more than 40 percent of their trash, while Americans recycle
just 10 percent of their greater waste output of 3.5 pounds
per person.

ON AN AVERAGE DAY...

Of the 144,000,000 pounds of solid waste that is not recycled,

... 97,920,000 pounds are incinerated

... 43,200,000 pounds are put into landfills

... 2,880,000 are composted

NOTE: The United States still sends more than 90 percent of its unrecycled waste to landfills.

ON AN AVERAGE DAY...

... 52,054,795 aluminum cans are produced

Of those,

... 34,356,164 are recycled

NOTE: Japan is currently recycling two-thirds of its food and beverage cans. The United States is recycling half of its cans, reusing 47,121,619 of the 93,310,137 cans it produces daily.

ON AN AVERAGE DAY...

... 151,376,301 pounds of paper are used
Of that,
... 75,688,151 pounds are recycled

NOTE: Japan reuses half of its paper. Americans, in contrast, recycle less than 30 percent of the 471,736,907 pounds of paper they use each day.

█ON AN AVERAGE DAY...

... 287,671 cubic meters of wood is consumed

Of that,

... 201,370 cubic meters must be imported

Of that,

... 57,534 cubic meters are taken from tropical forests

NOTE: The Japanese have come under mounting international pressure to limit their exploitation of tropical rainforests. Japan stands as the world's largest importer of tropical hardwood, accounting for 30 percent of the world's total imports. Most of this wood comes from the rainforests of Malaysia and New Guinea.

ON AN AVERAGE DAY...

... Japanese fisherman use harpoons and electric shock to kill 82 Dall's porpoises

NOTE: While fewer Japanese are eating whale-meat dishes, porpoise is gaining in favor as a delicacy in that country. Worldwide, it is estimated that 1.5 million dophins, porpoises, and small whales are killed each year by driftnets and harpoons.

ON AN AVERAGE DAY...

...54,931,507 pairs of "waribashi," or disposable chopsticks, are used once and then thrown away

Of those,

...27,397,260 are imported

NOTE: Japanese environmentalists have decried the use of disposable chopsticks. The wood used in the nation's "waribashi" account for .5 percent of Japan's total wood consumption.

ON AN AVERAGE DAY...

... Japanese spend $4,657,534 buying fur coats

NOTE: The anti-fur movement has not yet made its way into Japan. In contrast, fur sales in the United States are reported to be off as much as 50 percent.

ON AN AVERAGE DAY...

... Japanese families live with

... 6,000,000 cats

... 7,000,000 dogs

NOTE: Americans keep 50.5 million dogs and 57.9 million cats. Given the lack of available space in Japan, it is not surprising that Japanese favor smaller breeds of dogs.

ON AN AVERAGE DAY...

... Japanese live with 19,000,000 pet birds

NOTE: Probably in response to their close quarters, Japanese have taken to smaller pets. Americans, in contrast, have just 12,895,000 pet birds. Japanese also own a large number of pet insects (11,200,000), and pet fish (50,000,000).

ON AN AVERAGE DAY...

... Japanese maintain 217,701,000 religious affiliations

Including

... 111,792,000 who adhere to Shintoism

... 93,109,000 who are Buddhists

... 1,423,000 who are Christians

NOTE: The reason behind Japan's large number of religious affiliations (more than the number of its residents) is the fact that many Japanese adhere to both Shintoism and Buddhism.

ON AN AVERAGE DAY...

... 4,584 crimes are committed

... 1,177 Japanese are arrested

... 214 Japanese are sent to prison

NOTE: On an average day in the United States, 93,474 crimes are committed, 34,795 Americans are arrested, and 1,593 Americans are sent to prison. America's lower rate of incarceration comes as quite a surprise given the country's much higher incidence of serious crime.

ON AN AVERAGE DAY...

... 1,876 cars are stolen

... 462 bicycles are stolen

NOTE: In the United States, 3,926 cars and 1,015 bicycles are stolen each day.

ON AN AVERAGE DAY...

... 1 government official is arrested on corruption charges

... 35 Japanese are arrested for fraud

... 128 Japanese are arrested for embezzlement

NOTE: In the United States, 3 government officials are indicted on corruption charges, while 35 Americans are arrested for embezzlement and 957 are arrested for fraud.

ON AN AVERAGE DAY...

... 86,500 Japanese belong to one of Japan's "yakuza" (organized crime groups)

... organized crime takes in $25,479,452 in illegal receipts

NOTE: There are approximately 1,700 sworn Mafia members living in the United States. For each member, there are said to be at least 10 additional associates. While the number of gangsters in Japan has declined over the past 25 years, yakuza mambers still account for almost one-third of all the prisoners in Japanese jails.

ON AN AVERAGE DAY...

... 559 children are arrested

Of those,

... 236 are under fifteen years of age

... 4 are arrested for felonies

NOTE: Crime among America's youth has become pervasive. On an
average day, 4,477 American children are arrested. Of those,
1,446 are under the age of fifteen and 1,640 are arrested for
serious crimes.

ON AN AVERAGE DAY...

...59 children are arrested or given police guidance for the illegal use of drugs

NOTE: 212 American children are arrested for the possession, sale, or manufacture of illegal drugs.

ON AN AVERAGE DAY...

... 71 Japanese are arrested on drug-related charges

Of those,

... 46 are arrested for the possession, sale, or manufacture of stimulants

NOTE: 2,329 Americans are arrested each day for the possession, sale, or manufacture of illegal drugs. Drug violations have been rising steadily in the U.S. with the greatest number of arrests for the possession of heroin, cocaine, or marijuana.

ON AN AVERAGE DAY...

... police seize ...

... less than 1 pound of cocaine

... less than 1 pound of heroin

... 1 pound of speed

... 3 pounds of marijuana

NOTE: While the amount of illegal drugs confiscated by Japanese police is still quite small by international standards, government officials are concerned by a recent upward trend. Meanwhile, in the United States, officials seize 344 pounds of cocaine, 5 pounds of heroin, 3,244 pounds of marijuana, and 298,630 dosages of speed and LSD.

ON AN AVERAGE DAY...

... 8 Japanese are arrested on prostitution charges

... 11 Japanese are arrested on weapons possession charges

... 22 Japanese are arrested on gambling charges

NOTE: On an average day in the world's crime capital, 216 Americans are arrested on prostitution charges, 447 are arrested on weapons charges and 49 are arrested on gambling charges.

ON AN AVERAGE DAY...

... 5 Japanese are robbed

NOTE: On an average day in the United States, 1,491 Americans are robbed.

🛕ON AN AVERAGE DAY...

... 5 Japanese are raped

NOTE: On an average day in the United States, 254 Americans are raped.

ON AN AVERAGE DAY...

... 4 Japanese are murdered

NOTE: On an average day in the United States, 57 Americans are murdered.

ON AN AVERAGE DAY...

...45,736 persons are serving time in
Japanese prisons

Of those,

...43,845 are men

...1,891 are women

NOTE: In the United States, 627,402 persons are serving time in
prison. Of those, 594,711 are men and 32,691 are women.
The U.S. has the highest incarceration rate of any country
while Japan ranks among the lowest.

ON AN AVERAGE DAY...

... 80 Japanese are on "death row"

NOTE: More than 2,000 Americans are on "death row." While
capital punishment is legal in Japan, no executions were
carried out in 1990 (for the first time in 22 years). The only
accepted method of capital punishment in Japan is by
hanging, while Americans may be terminated by lethal
injection, electrocution, lethal gas, hanging, or firing squad.

ON AN AVERAGE DAY...

... 16,608 workers are "known" to be in the country illegally

Of those,

... 11,791 are men

... 4,817 are women

NOTE: Unofficial estimates put the number of illegal workers in Japan at between 200,000 and 300,000. Of those, an estimated 100,000 are working in the sex and entertainment industry, 50,000 in manufacturing, 50,000 in construction, and 30,000 in service industries. It is widely believed that the Japanese government has not yet allowed itself to acknowledge this growing problem.

ON AN AVERAGE DAY...

... of the 11,917 males working illegally in Japan,

... 5,589 are working in the construction industry

... 4,693 are working in factories

... 578 are working at odd jobs

... 224 are working as shop clerks

☖ON AN AVERAGE DAY...

... of the 4,817 females working illegally in Japan,

... 3,227 are working as bar hostesses

... 323 are working in factories

... 275 are working at odd jobs

... 178 are working as prostitutes

... 154 are working as house maids

... 154 are working as stripteasers

... 140 are working as shop clerks

ON AN AVERAGE DAY...

... 62,700,000 Japanese are employed

Of those,

... 12,227,000 are members of labor unions

NOTE: Of America's 116,677,000 workers, 17,002,000 are members of unions. Union membership has been in decline in both Japan and the United States.

ON AN AVERAGE DAY...

... 1,420,000 Japanese are unemployed

NOTE: In the United States, nearly 7,000,000 Americans are unemployed. While Japan's 1.4 million unemployed may sound like a large number of people, it only represents 2.3 percent of the population, while America's unemployment rate hovers around the 7 percent level.

ON AN AVERAGE DAY...

... 603 Japanese workers are on strike

NOTE: On an average day in the United States, 11,956 American
workers are on strike. The number of strikers in both Japan
and the U.S. has declined in recent years.

🏯ON AN AVERAGE DAY...

...there is a shortage of 1,900,000
workers

NOTE: There are an average of 1.3 job openings for each job-seeker
in Japan. Hardest hit are the construction industry, with
25.9 percent of jobs unfilled; service, with 10.1 percent; and
manufacturing, with 9.6 percent. As a result, the government
has been under pressure to relax its immigration restrictions.

▲ON AN AVERAGE DAY...

... the workforce grows by 2,849 persons
   Of those,
... 1,205 are men
... 1,644 are women

NOTE: The American workforce grows by 4,942 persons. Of those,
      1,973 are men and 2,969 are women. Women now comprise
      over 40 percent of Japan's workforce while they make up
      45 percent of the American labor pool. In both countries, the
      number of working women has grown steadily.

ON AN AVERAGE DAY...

... the number of Japanese employed in
farming decreases by 307 persons

... the number of Japanese employed in
the service industries increases by
142 persons

NOTE: The United States is also experiencing a shift away from
farming and toward the service industries. On an average
day, the number of Americans involved in agriculture shrinks
by 107 persons. Meanwhile, the number of persons employed
in the service industries grows by 3,562.

ON AN AVERAGE DAY...

... more than 500,000 Japanese are
   employed as Amway distributors

   Of those,

... 300,000 are women

... 200,000 are men

   Together, they sell ...

... $1,523,014 worth of Amway products

NOTE: Though Amway has been in Japan for just 11 years, its sales
   there are expected to pass those in the United States in the
   very near future. Worldwide, more than 1 million individuals
   sell $3.1 billion worth of Amway products, each year, in more
   than 50 countries and territories.

ON AN AVERAGE DAY...

... work accidents cause

... 6 deaths

... 615 serious injuries

NOTE: In the United States, work accidents cause 29 deaths and
4,932 serious injuries.

ON AN AVERAGE DAY...

...the average worker spends 42
minutes commuting to and from work

NOTE: The average American worker spends 41 minutes commuting
to and from work.

ON AN AVERAGE DAY...

... the average worker spends 5 hours and 53 minutes at work (average over 7 days each week)

NOTE: The average American workers spends 5 hours and 16 minutes working (average over 7 days each week). At some 2,150 hours, the Japanese work year stands among the world's longest.

ON AN AVERAGE DAY...

...2 "karoshi" (death from overwork) cases are filed

NOTE: The number of karoshi cases has been increasing at the rate of 35 percent each year. Of the 777 cases filed in 1988, however, only 30 were granted compensation. Experts estimate that the actual number of cases exceeds 10,000 each year.

ON AN AVERAGE DAY...

...5,999,000 Japanese would like to
leave their present jobs

Of those,

...7,249 do so

NOTE: The Japanese are known for their devotion to their
employers. This lifelong commitment, however, is rapidly
becoming just a symbol of the past. As evidence of this, the
number of Japanese who change jobs each day has grown 75
percent over the past five years.

ON AN AVERAGE DAY...

... 159 persons emigrate from Japan

... 236 persons immigrate to Japan

NOTE: On an average day, 1,648 persons immigrate to the United
States while an estimated 438 persons emigrate to other
countries.

ON AN AVERAGE DAY...

... 984,455 citizens of other countries are living in Japan

Of those,

... 681,838 are from Korea

... 137,499 are from China

... 38,925 are from the Philippines

... 34,900 are from the United States

NOTE: More than 14 million foreign-born persons are living in the United States. Countries having the greatest number of residents in the U.S. include (in order of most residents): Mexico, Canada, Germany, Italy, Cuba, the Philippines, England, and the Soviet Union.

ON AN AVERAGE DAY...

... 548,404 Japanese are residing in other countries

Of those,

... 189,856 are living in the United States

... 112,979 are living in Brazil

... 31,162 are living in England

... 19,827 are living in Germany

... 19,620 are living in Canada

NOTE: More than 2 million Americans are residing in other countries. Of those, the greatest number are in Mexico, Canada, England, the Philippines, and Germany.

🏯 ON AN AVERAGE DAY...

... 41,347 foreign students are studying at Japanese institutions

Of those,

... 1,180 are Americans

NOTE: More than 366,000 foreign students are studying at American colleges and universities. Of those, 24,000 are from Japan.

ON AN AVERAGE DAY...

... Japanese school-age children spend an average of ...

... 7 hours and 1 minute in school (school day)

... 2 hours and 4 minutes doing homework

NOTE: American school-age children spend an average of 5 hours and 20 minutes in school (school day) and 25 minutes doing homework. Japanese children attend school six days each week.

ON AN AVERAGE DAY...

... Japanese school-age children spend an average of ...

... 44 minutes playing games and sports

... 8 hours and 17 minutes sleeping

NOTE: American school-age children spend an average of 1 hour and 27 minutes playing games and sports, and 8 hours and 57 minutes sleeping.

ON AN AVERAGE DAY...

... Japanese school-age children spend an average of ...

... 25 minutes reading

... 2 hours and 17 minutes watching television

NOTE: The average American school-age child spends 11 minutes reading and 2 hours and 15 minutes watching television.

ON AN AVERAGE DAY...

... 337 children drop out of school

NOTE: In the United States, 915 children drop out of school. The
number of Japanese students who drop out represents an
increase of 5.5 percent over last year's number.

ON AN AVERAGE DAY...

...the average Japanese man spends
2 minutes on childcare

...the average Japanese woman spends
27 minutes on childcare

NOTE: The average American man spends 7 minutes on childcare
while the average woman spends 27 minutes.

ON AN AVERAGE DAY...

... the average Japanese man spends
9 minutes cleaning house

... the average Japanese woman spends
3 hours and 1 minute cleaning house

NOTE: American men are not much better when it comes to sharing
the housecleaning burden. American men spend an average
of 26 minutes cleaning house while their female counterparts
spend 59 minutes.

ON AN AVERAGE DAY...

... the average Japanese man spends
7 minutes shopping

... the average Japanese woman spends
32 minutes shopping

NOTE: American men spend 20 minutes shopping while women
spend 38 minutes.

☗ON AN AVERAGE DAY...

... the average Japanese spends 3 hours and 23 minutes watching television

... the average Japanese spends 40 minutes listening to the radio

NOTE: Americans spend an average of 4 hours and 17 minutes watching television and a considerable 3 hours listening to their radios. America's greater dependence on their automobiles is the driving force behind the country's deeper connection with the radio medium.

ON AN AVERAGE DAY...

... $93,087,460 is spent on advertising
   Of that,
... $27,740,063 is spent on television
... $23,737,302 is spent on newspapers
... $6,516,122 is spent on billboards
... $6,236,860 is spent on magazines
... $4,002,761 is spent on radio

NOTE: The United States is by far the world's leader when it comes
   to advertising. On an average day, marketers spend
   $323,424,658 trying to influence the country's buying
   decisions. Favorite media are newspapers, magazines,
   television, direct mail, yellow pages, and radio.

⛩ON AN AVERAGE DAY...

... 394,521 Japanese go to the movies

... movie attendance decreases by 2,740 persons

NOTE: Both the number of Japanese movie theaters and the number attending have been in decline. In contrast, moviegoing in the United States has remained fairly steady, with 2,824,658 persons attending films daily.

ON AN AVERAGE DAY...

... 1,171 new homes are wired for cable
television

NOTE: In the United States, 10,759 new homes are wired for cable
television. A relative newcomer to Japan (with fewer than
20 percent of homes wired), cable television is catching on
quickly. As was true in the United States, cable television in
Japan was originally developed to provide television coverage
to areas with poor reception.

ON AN AVERAGE DAY...

... 19,603 VCRs are purchased

NOTE: Americans purchase 33,003 VCRs. With U.S. VCR penetration reaching 70 percent, a growing proportion of sales are replacement units or upgrades to stereo sound or higher performance. VCR penetration in Japan is also approaching 70 percent.

ON AN AVERAGE DAY...

... 2,157,534 videos are rented

... 41,952 videos are purchased

NOTE: Americans rent 6,301,370 videos and buy 731,507.

ON AN AVERAGE DAY...

... 71,500,000 newspapers are purchased

NOTE: The Japanese read more newspapers per capita than the people of any other nation. It is estimated that 90 percent of Japanese read a newspaper every day. Americans, on the other hand, purchase just 63 million newspapers, while 60 percent of Americans read a newspaper daily.

ON AN AVERAGE DAY...

... 11,617,644 magazines are purchased

NOTE: Americans have a much stronger affinity for magazines,
purchasing approximately 80 million issues daily.

♨ON AN AVERAGE DAY...

... 750 foreign news correspondents are
   in Japan covering national events

   Of those,

... 259 are from the United States

NOTE: Japanese news organizations maintain 492 correspondents
   overseas. Of those, 167 are stationed in the United States.

☖ON AN AVERAGE DAY...

... 4,657,534 comic books are purchased

Of those,

... 1,571,068 are bought by adults

NOTE: Comic books, or "manga" as they are called in Japan, are a national favorite. It is not uncommon for a special issue of a particular comic to sell several million copies.

ON AN AVERAGE DAY...

... 101 new book titles are published
Of those,

... 25 concern the social sciences

... 19 are fiction

... 9 concern engineering

... 8 concern art

... 8 concern the applied sciences

... 8 are children's books

... 6 concern history

... 5 concern philosophy

... 5 concern business

... 4 are general interest

NOTE: In the United States, 124 new books are published. Of those, 22 concern sociology and economics, 15 are fiction, 10 are children's, 9 concern medicine, 8 concern the natural sciences, 6 concern religion, 6 are general interest, and 4 concern the arts.

ON AN AVERAGE DAY...

... Japanese send 58,892,277 pieces of mail

Of those,

... 332,704 are sent to international destinations

NOTE: Americans send 439,701,370 pieces of mail. Of those, 1,972,603 are sent to international destinations. Part of the explanation for Japan's lower per capita mailing rate lies in their limited involvement with junk mail. Japanese also prefer to pay their bills with bank transfers as opposed to checks.

# ON AN AVERAGE DAY...

... Japanese purchase 219 cellular
telephones

NOTE: Perhaps as a result of their greater dependence on
automobiles, Americans purchase more than four times as
many cellular telephones as the Japanese. On an average day,
907 Americans make the move to a cellular system. In total,
more than 5 million Americans subscribe to cellular phone
systems versus fewer than 1 million Japanese.

ON AN AVERAGE DAY...

... Japanese make 187,123,288 domestic
   telephone calls

   Of those,

... 93,000,274 last a minute or less

NOTE: Americans love to talk on the telephone, making an average
      of 1,662,000,000 domestic calls each business day.

ON AN AVERAGE DAY...

... Japanese make 367,463 international telephone calls

NOTE: Americans make 997,466 international telephone calls each day.

🗼ON AN AVERAGE DAY...

... 144,617,871 gallons of oil are
imported

Including

... 98,924,340 gallons that are imported
from the Middle East

NOTE: The United States imports 175,476,000 gallons of oil each
day. Of that, 33,768,000 gallons come from the Middle East.
While the United States remains dependent on foreign
countries for much of its oil, Japan is almost completely
dependent on foreign suppliers.

ON AN AVERAGE DAY...

... 4,981,096 barrels of oil are used

... 543,000,000 barrels of oil are in reserves

Including

... 140,000,000 barrels that are stockpiled by the government

NOTE: The United States uses 17,324,932 barrels of oil each day. The country has reserves of 1.5 billion barrels, including 595 million barrels stockpiled by the government. At present levels, Japan has 132 days of reserves and the U.S. has 99.

ON AN AVERAGE DAY...

...61 percent of the country's electricity is supplied by coal

...28 percent of the country's electricity is supplied by nuclear power

NOTE: Both Japan and the United States obtain a majority of their electricity from coal. Nuclear is the second greatest source for both countries with the U.S. getting just under 20 percent of its electricity from this source. Other major sources of electricity are gas, hydroelectric, and petroleum.

♠ON AN AVERAGE DAY...

... the government spends $107,397,260
on defense

NOTE: The United States is the world's leader when it comes to
defense spending, paying $795,342,466 each day to maintain
its military might.

ON AN AVERAGE DAY...

... the government spends $8,219,178 to keep 50,000 American troops stationed in Japan

NOTE: Japan currently contributes just 40 percent of the total cost of stationing U.S. troops in its country. With mounting fiscal and political pressure in the U.S., however, the Japanese government has agreed to increase its share of the cost to at least one-half.

ON AN AVERAGE DAY...

... $1,986,301 worth of military arms are imported

Including

... $751,233 that comes from the United States

NOTE: The United States also imports arms, $7,219,178 worth each day. The U.S., however, is also a major arms exporter, selling $149,698,630 worth of military equipment and weapons each day.

ON AN AVERAGE DAY...

... 244,000 Japanese are on active duty
in the armed forces

NOTE: The United States has approximately 2,279,000 soldiers on
active duty. On a per capita basis, the U.S. has nearly five
times as many of its citizens in the military.

ON AN AVERAGE DAY...

... the government gives $24,520,548 in aid to foreign countries

NOTE: For the first time, Japan surpassed the U.S. in terms of foreign aid. The U.S. gives $20,986,301 each day. Japan, however, has been criticized for attaching conditions to its aid and limiting its distribution to neighboring Asian countries or those that are willing to use the funds to buy Japanese goods and services.

ON AN AVERAGE DAY...

... 2 refugees are granted political
asylum in Japan

NOTE: With more than 13 million refugees around the world
seeking asylum from persecution or violence, wealthier
nations are feeling increased pressure from the international
community to help out. The United States has been very
active in the resettlement of refugees, with an average of 192
accepted daily. Japan, on the other hand, has generally been
less active in this arena.

132

ON AN AVERAGE DAY...

... 62 foreigners are deported from the
country

NOTE: In the United States, 2,567 foreign citizens are forced to
leave the country. While most of Japan's illegal visitors come
from Korea, most of America's illegal entrants arrive from
Mexico.

ON AN AVERAGE DAY...

... the world's 8 largest banks are based in Japan

... 33 of the world's 100 largest banks are based in Japan

NOTE: Only America's Citicorp makes it into the world's top 10 banks (by total assets), at number 9. Of the world's 100 largest banks, only 9 are American.

ON AN AVERAGE DAY...

... 20 businesses declare bankruptcy

NOTE: U.S. corporations declare bankruptcy at the rate of 150 each day. Labor shortages in Japan have been blamed for the recent increase in the number of manufacturing and construction failures, while the country's restrictive monetary policy has been blamed for the recent rise in real estate failures.

ON AN AVERAGE DAY...

... 962 patent applications are received by the Japanese government

Of those,

... 82 are received from foreign governments, companies, and individuals

Of those,

... 35 come from the United States

... 16 come from Germany

... 5 come from France

... 5 come from England

NOTE: The United States receives 416 patent applications and awards 231. Of those, 109 are issued to foreign countries. Tops among those countries are Japan (47), Germany (21), France (8), and England (8).

ON AN AVERAGE DAY...

... the government awards 328 trademarks

Of those,

... 27 are awarded to foreign governments, businesses, and individuals

NOTE: The U.S. government awards 148 trademarks. Of those, 24 are issued to foreign applicants.

ON AN AVERAGE DAY...

... $223,974,710 is spent on research and development

Of that,

... $179,167,545 comes from private-sector funding sources

NOTE: Japan's R&D spending is second only to that of the U.S. The U.S. spends $382,718,651 on research and development daily. What is interesting to note is that just over half of American spending comes from private-sector sources. In contrast, Japan has shown that its corporations are not going to wait around for the government to fund its research.

ON AN AVERAGE DAY...

... businesses spend $1,504,109,589 on "capital investment" (new factories and industrial equipment)

NOTE: For the first time since World War II, a country other than the U.S. is the world's leader in capital investment. The United States now ranks second with $1,405,479,452 invested in plants and equipment each day. Capital investment is widely believed to be the most important factor in determining a country's future productivity and standard of living.

ON AN AVERAGE DAY...

... American companies invest
$4,860,274 in Japan

... Japanese companies invest
$44,783,562 in the United States

NOTE: While U.S. investments in Japan have been growing for
several years, they pale in comparison with the activity of
Japanese companies in the U.S. More than 80 percent of
Japan's investments are in real estate. In terms of total
cumulative investments in the U.S., Japan stands second to
Great Britain.

≜ON AN AVERAGE DAY...

... Japanese corporations spend
$29,041,096 taking over foreign
companies

Of that,

... $20,821,918 is spent taking over
American companies

NOTE: American companies spend an average of $38,356,164 taking
over foreign firms. Of that, $20,273,973 is spent taking over
Japanese companies. Surprisingly, and in spite of all of the
attention that accompanies any Japanese purchase of any
U.S. company, Japan is not the world's leading purchaser of
American businesses. British and French corporations place
number one and two, respectively, in the takeover of
American companies.

ON AN AVERAGE DAY...

... Japanese companies add 91
   Americans to their U.S.
   manufacturing workforces

NOTE: While increasing at a steady rate, less than 5 percent of
   Japan's manufacturing is done overseas. By contrast,
   American companies do 18 percent of their manufacturing in
   other countries.

ON AN AVERAGE DAY...

... $610,727,081 worth of goods are imported

... $797,112,750 worth of goods are exported

NOTE: In contrast to Japan, the U.S. has a trade deficit. On an average day, the U.S. imports $1,207,945,205 worth of goods while it exports just $882,739,726.

ON AN AVERAGE DAY...

... $1,369,863 worth of toys are imported

... $2,170,706 worth of toys are exported

NOTE: Unlike Japan, the United States is a net importer of toys. The U.S. imports $15,252,055 and exports $1,027,397 worth of toys each day.

♨ON AN AVERAGE DAY...

... $113,551,107 worth of goods are
imported into Japan from the United
States

... $242,086,407 worth of goods are
exported to the United States

NOTE: Since 1980, Japan has enjoyed a trade surplus with the
United States. The top U.S. export categories to Japan
include aerospace, computers, lumber, corn, and art and
antiques. The top Japanese exports to the U.S. include motor
vehicles, computers, telecommunications equipment, and
consumer electronics.

ON AN AVERAGE DAY...

... $31,490 worth of cosmetics are imported into Japan from the United States

... $108,013 worth of cosmetics are exported to the United States

ON AN AVERAGE DAY...

... 86,290 VCRs are produced

Of those,

... 59,899 are exported

Of those,

... 26,016 are exported to the United States

NOTE: Japan imports just over 1,000 VCRs each day.

ON AN AVERAGE DAY...

... 24,932 new cars are manufactured

Of those,

... 11,233 are exported

Of those,

... 4,658 are exported to the United States

NOTE: Japan is the world's leading producer of motor vehicles, accounting for more than 1 in 4 of the world's new cars. Following Japan are the United States, West Germany, France, the Soviet Union, Italy, Canada, the United Kingdom, Korea, and Brazil. Japan imports just 97 cars each day from the U.S.

ON AN AVERAGE DAY...

... 12,329 new cars are purchased

Of those,

... 555 are imports

Of those,

... 107 are Mercedes

... 101 are Volkswagens

... 100 are BMWs

... 46 are Audis

... 40 are Rovers

... 30 are Volvos

... 23 are General Motors

... 21 are Hondas (built in the U.S.)

NOTE: The number of foreign cars sold in Japan has been increasing. The number sold, however, is dwarfed by the number of Japanese cars sold in other countries.

ON AN AVERAGE DAY...

... 219,700 robots are working in industry

NOTE: Japan is by far the world's leading employer of industrial robots, utilizing nearly 70 percent of the world's total. The United States ranks second, with 32,600 robots in use.

ON AN AVERAGE DAY...

... 120 robots are added to the active
industrial population

NOTE: In the United States, just 14 robots are added to the
industrial population each day. Driven by severe labor
shortages and labor-management cooperation, Japan is
utilizing robots in a wide range of endeavors. Japanese
robots paint walls, pour and smooth concrete, transplant
flowers and even set up folding chairs in auditoriums.

🌲ON AN AVERAGE DAY...

... the average chief executive officer (CEO) earns 17 times as much as the average worker

NOTE: Increasingly, CEOs in the U.S. have been criticized for their excessive compensation packages, sometime reaching into the hundreds of millions of dollars. The average U.S. chief executive officer earns 85 times what the average worker takes home.

ON AN AVERAGE DAY...

... corporations donate $2,479,452 to not-for-profit organizations

NOTE: Japanese corporate giving pales in comparison to that in the United States. Corporations in the U.S. give more than $13 million to charities each day.

ON AN AVERAGE DAY...

... corporations spend $1,547,945 on
support for the arts

NOTE: While corporate support for the arts is a relatively new
phenomenon in Japan, it has grown rapidly. American
companies have long recognized the public relations value of
supporting arts groups and events. On an average day,
American companies spend $1,917,808 in support for the
arts. As with American companies, Japanese support goes
predominantly to established or more recognized art groups
and events and ignores the developing arts and artists.

ON AN AVERAGE DAY...

... the government spends $7,123,288 in support for the arts

Of that,

... $6,164,384 is spent by local governments

... $958,904 is spent by the federal government

NOTE: In the U.S., the states and federal government are much less supportive of the arts. On an average day, state governments spend $665,321 and the federal government spends $811,781 on support for the arts.

ON AN AVERAGE DAY...

...the poorest 20 percent of the population takes home 9 percent of the country's earnings

...the wealthiest 20 percent of the population takes home 37 percent of the country's national income

NOTE: Despite what at first may appear to be a very inequitable sharing of wealth in Japan, the U.S. is even worse. The poorest 20 percent of Americans hold just 4 percent of the nation's income, while the wealthiest 20 percent control 46 percent. Japan's equity ratio (share of richest to share of poorest) is among the world's best, following that of China and the Soviet Union.

♟ON AN AVERAGE DAY...

... 3,390,000 Japanese are involved in volunteer work

... the number of Japanese involved in volunteer work grows by 1,370

NOTE: With its new wealth has come a brand new sense of community in Japan. The United States has long had a strong spirit of volunteerism, with more than 81 million Americans involved in some kind of volunteer activity.

ON AN AVERAGE DAY...

...21,847 Japanese donate blood

NOTE: As is true in Japan, only 6 percent of Americans donate blood each year. On an average day, 48,219 Americans donate some of their blood.

ON AN AVERAGE DAY...

... the average Japanese household takes in $135

Of that,

... $16 is put into savings

NOTE: The Japanese are known for their high rate of savings. The average American household, meanwhile, takes in an average of $118 each day and puts only $4 of that into savings.

ON AN AVERAGE DAY...

... the average Japanese has $40,119 in his or her bank savings accounts

NOTE: In contrast to the Japanese, the average American has just $10,822 in his or her bank savings accounts.

ON AN AVERAGE DAY...

... 40 of the world's 270 billionaires live
   in Japan

NOTE: Japan trails only the United States in this category. And
      while 99 Americans may be billionaires, Japan has 2
      residents worth more than $10 billion, while the United
      States has none.

ON AN AVERAGE DAY...

... 170,000,000 credit cards are in circulation

... and growing at the rate of ...

... 82,192 cards a day

NOTE: Americans carry more than 860 million credit cards. They add 381,151 new cards to their arsenal every day.

ON AN AVERAGE DAY...

... Japanese spend $3,102,509,589
   Of that,

... $164,383,562 is charged to credit
   cards

NOTE: Of the $7,669,410,962 Americans spend each day, they say
"charge it!" to the tune of $1,087,945,205.

ON AN AVERAGE DAY...

... Japanese spend $27,608,008 buying
products through mail order

NOTE: While still a relatively young industry in Japan, direct-mail
orders are growing at the rate of $3,371,970 each day.
Americans, on the other hand, have become experts at
shopping from home, spending more than $272 million each
day.

ON AN AVERAGE DAY...

... Japanese spend $118,630,137 buying products from vending machines

NOTE: There are more than 5 million vending machines in Japan today, about the same number as in the U.S., but serving about half as many people. Americans also spend less on the machines than the Japanese—parting with just $62,924,081 each day. Reasons behind the greater role of vending machines in Japan include: a greater variety of available products—including flowers, rice, frozen beef, videocassettes, and pornography; a safer environment against potential theft and vandalism; a national acceptance of technology; and a demonstrated desire for greater convenience.

ON AN AVERAGE DAY...

... Japanese spend $204,833,149 on
   clothing

   Of that,

... $14,445,297 is spent on kimonos
   (traditional Japanese robes)

ON AN AVERAGE DAY...

... the average Japanese spends $19 on living expenses

Of that,

... $5.05 is spent on food

... $2.09 is spent on housing

NOTE: The average American spends $26 each day on living expenses. Of that, $3.87 is spent on food and $6.14 is spent on housing. Japanese spend a much higher percentage of their living expenses on food because so much of the country's food must be imported.

☗ON AN AVERAGE DAY...

... Japanese shop at 1,619,599 retail
  stores

  Of those,

... 547,424 are food stores

  Of those,

... 127,948 specialize in fresh produce

NOTE: When it comes to buying their food, the Japanese want it
     fresh. Americans rely to a greater extent on frozen and
     packaged foods. Of the 1,508,828 retail stores in the United
     States, 241,412 sell food products and just 22,632 specialize
     in fresh foods. Japanese stores also tend to be much smaller
     than those in America.

168

ON AN AVERAGE DAY...

... the average Japanese consumes
  2,620 calories

... the average Japanese consumes
  81 grams of fat

NOTE: While the fat intake of the average Japanese has gone up in
recent years, they still eat more healthfully than their
American counterparts. On an average day, Americans
consume 3,546 calories and 178 grams of fat.

ON AN AVERAGE DAY...

... Japanese eat 63,779,882 pounds of fish

NOTE: The Japanese are by far the world's leading consumers of seafood. Meanwhile, Americans eat just 24,700,387 pounds of fish daily. On a per capita basis, the average Japanese eats more than 8 ounces of fish each day while Americans eat less than 2 ounces.

ON AN AVERAGE DAY...

... Japanese eat 51,804,334 pounds of rice

... the amount of rice eaten declines by 112,131 pounds

NOTE: While the amount of rice eaten in the United States has been increasing, Americans still only consume 9 million pounds of rice each day.

ON AN AVERAGE DAY...

... Japanese eat 12,602,740 servings of "ramen" (a fast-food noodle dish originated in Japan more than 30 years ago)

NOTE: People worldwide eat 14 billion servings of "ramen" each year. Japan is the largest consumer, buying 4.6 billion servings annually.

ON AN AVERAGE DAY...

... Japanese eat 7,194,916 pounds of frozen food

NOTE: Americans consume much more frozen food than the Japanese. On a daily basis, Americans eat 72,916,758 pounds of frozen food.

ON AN AVERAGE DAY...

...Japanese eat 5,718,660 pounds of red meat

NOTE: While Japanese consumption of red meat has doubled since the early seventies, it still pales in comparison to the United States. Americans eat more than 70 million pounds of red meat each day. On a per capita basis, Japanese eat less than 1 ounce each day, while Americans consume almost 5 ounces daily.

ON AN AVERAGE DAY...

... 1,600,000 Japanese eat at McDonald's

NOTE: Of the nearly 134 million Americans who eat a meal out of the home each day, 16.3 million choose to eat at McDonald's. In addition to Big Macs, the Japanese have also taken a liking to Kentucky Fried Chicken (900 outlets), Domino's Pizza (61 stores), Dairy Queen (121 stores), and Baskin-Robbins (439 stores). They also visit 7-Eleven stores to the tune of 4,000,000 customers each day.

175

ON AN AVERAGE DAY...

... Japanese drink 61,896,088 cups of coffee

... Japanese drink 97,419,060 cups of tea

NOTE: The consumption of coffee in Japan has doubled over the past ten years. Americans, despite some loss in their affection for coffee over recent years, still drink more than 286 million cups daily. Consumption of tea in the U.S. has remained steady at about 76 millions cups per day.

ON AN AVERAGE DAY...

... Japanese drink 5,394,231 gallons of alcoholic beverages

Including,

... 3,549,404 gallons of beer

... 997,933 gallons of sake

... 415,356 gallons of shochu (a rice-based liquor)

... 194,192 gallons of whisky

... 64,731 gallons of wine

NOTE: Americans also love beer the best. On an average day, Americans guzzle 23,215,665 gallons of beer. They also drink 2,294,572 gallons of wine and 1,552,210 gallons of liquor.

ON AN AVERAGE DAY...

...Japanese buy...

...46,200 sets of golf clubs

...435,518 golf balls

NOTE: On an average day, Americans purchase 33,973 sets of golf clubs and 486,575 golf balls.

🏯 ON AN AVERAGE DAY...

... Japan exports 76,044 golf balls to the United States

... Japan imports 128,022 golf balls from the United States

☗ON AN AVERAGE DAY...

... 27,000,000 Japanese consider
themselves to be golfers

Of those,

... 12,000,000 have never played on a
real golf course

NOTE: While fewer Americans than Japanese play golf (23,000,000),
they are generally more successful in their attempts to play
on golf courses. Meanwhile, more than 5,000,000 of
America's golfers are women, while just 2,500,000 Japanese
women have taken up the sport.

ON AN AVERAGE DAY...

... 445,477 Japanese play golf at a "real" course

... 827,496 Japanese visit golf practice ranges

NOTE: The Japanese are golfing fanatics. Unfortunately, due to a shortage of golf courses in the country, most have never actually played on a golf course. Of the country's 1,600 golf courses, only a few hundred are open to the public—and those have people waiting through the night. Lifetime memberships at private clubs can go for as much as $3,000,000.

ON AN AVERAGE DAY...

... 6 new golf holes are constructed

NOTE: On an average day, 14 new golf holes are constructed in the United States.

ON AN AVERAGE DAY...

... Japanese businesses invest $1,826,484 in American golf courses.

NOTE: It is estimated that Japanese companies own or have interests in approximately 160 American golf courses. Included in Japan's portfolio is the prestigious Pebble Beach Golf Club in California.

ON AN AVERAGE DAY...

... Japanese spend $40,042,150 on golf

... Japanese spend $224,657,534 playing pachinko (a Japanese form of pinball)

ON AN AVERAGE DAY...

... Japanese spend $8,472,076 on toys
   Of that,
... $2,287,460 is spent on video games

NOTE: On an average day, Americans spend $31,268,493 on toys. As in Japan, the largest category is video games with $6,657,534 in sales.

ON AN AVERAGE DAY...

... Japanese travel 69,756,164 miles by air (domestic)

... Japanese travel 852,386,301 miles by car

NOTE: On an average day, Americans travel 902,191,781 miles by air (domestic) and 3,706,849,315 miles by car.

ON AN AVERAGE DAY...

... Japanese take 311,395 airplane trips
Of those,
... 25,923 are taken on international
routes

NOTE: Americans take 1,246,575 airplane trips. Of those, 95,890 are
flown on international routes.

ON AN AVERAGE DAY...

... 26,473 Japanese leave to visit other countries

Of those,

... 2,149 visit Korea

... 1,467 visit the United States

... 1,364 visit Taiwan

... 472 visit England

... 171 visit Germany

... 163 visit Canada

NOTE: 39,805 Americans leave on trips to other countries. Favorite destinations include England, Japan, Mexico, Germany, the Bahamas, and France.

ON AN AVERAGE DAY...

... 7,767 tourists travel to Japan
   Of those,
... 1,671 come from Korea
... 1,457 come from the United States
... 1,446 come from Taiwan
... 486 come from England
... 269 come from China

NOTE: 96,573 tourists enter the U.S. each day. Leading countries of origin are Canada (42,098), Japan (8,439), England (6,087), Mexico (3,401) and Germany (2,949).

ON AN AVERAGE DAY...

... tourists spend $20,232,877 while
visiting Japan

... Japanese tourists spend $51,240,548
while visiting other countries

NOTE: The United States takes in $50,482,192 in tourist revenues
while Americans spend $80,576,438 while visiting other
countries.

ON AN AVERAGE DAY...

... 478,080 persons visit one of Japan's
amusement parks

NOTE: On an average day, 643,836 persons visit one of America's
amusement parks.

ON AN AVERAGE DAY...

... 32,877 persons visit Tokyo Disneyland
And while there they spend ...
... $1,871,460 ($57 per person)

NOTE: Disney's most popular U.S. attraction, Disney World in
Florida, receives 78,082 visitors daily. California's Disneyland
attracts 35,342 visitors each day—just slightly more than its
Japanese counterpart.

☗ON AN AVERAGE DAY...

... 1,028,663 persons visit one of Japan's 28 national parks

... the amount of land included in the country's national parks system increases by 32 acres

NOTE: Just 154,521 persons visit one of America's 50 national parks. Meanwhile, the amount of land dedicated to the National Parks System grows by 581 acres.

ON AN AVERAGE DAY...

... 356,164 Japanese visit one of the country's 2,000 "onsen" (hot-springs) resorts

NOTE: "Onsen" are considered to be the rural hot-springs cousin of the Japanese "sento" (public bath). With the rapid rise in the installation of indoor bathing facilities in Japanese homes, however, the number of sento has dwindled to just under 11,000.

ON AN AVERAGE DAY...

... 169,485 Japanese visit museums
   Of those,
... 59,416 visit art museums

NOTE: 966,400 Americans visit museums. Of those, 113,564 visit art museums.

ON AN AVERAGE DAY...

... 1,582,820 Japanese visit one of the country's 15,000 pachinko parlors (pinball parlors which offer prizes to winners)

NOTE: Japanese laws prohibit the awarding of cash prizes to winners but patrons simply take their prizes to local stores which exchange them for cash. Pachinko operators have traditionally been major contributors to the country's political parties.

☗ON AN AVERAGE DAY...

... Japanese buy 28,178 new cameras

... Japanese take 23,816,538 pictures
   Of those,

... 17,386,073 are taken with Fuji film

... 4,048,811 are taken with Konica film

... 2,381,654 are taken with Kodak film

NOTE: Americans buy 51,233 new cameras. They also take 41,506,849 pictures. Of those, 33,205,479 are taken with Kodak film and 4,150,685 are taken with Fuji film.

ON AN AVERAGE DAY...

...549,554 Japanese go bowling

NOTE: Bowling has been growing in popularity in Japan over the past few years. In the United States, Americans also love to bowl, visiting their local lanes 2,100,822 times each day.

ON AN AVERAGE DAY...

... 214,457 Japanese adults participate in traditional Japanese dancing

... 265,467 Japanese adults participate in traditional Western-style dancing (ballroom dancing, square-dancing, etc.)

NOTE: The Japanese continue to show their affection for things Western.

ON AN AVERAGE DAY...

... 765,689 Japanese adults sing along to taped music using their karaoke machines

NOTE: A popular fad in Japan for several years, karaoke is catching on in the U.S. as well, with many bars now featuring the sing-along machines.

ON AN AVERAGE DAY...

... Japanese purchase 601,644
prerecorded audiotapes, CDs, and
records

NOTE: On an average day, Americans purchase 2,194,247
prerecorded audiotapes, CDs, and records. As is true in the
U.S., CDs are the fastest growing prerecorded music category
in Japan.

ON AN AVERAGE DAY...

... Japanese purchase 72,055 "heated carpets"

NOTE: Manufactured only in Japan, heated carpets are used by nearly half of the Japanese people.

▲ ON AN AVERAGE DAY...

...Japanese purchase 13,111,781 flowers
Of those,

...4,825,135 are chrysanthemums

...1,888,096 are carnations

...996,495 are roses

NOTE: Americans purchase 9,448,236 flowers daily. On a per capita basis, Japan is the world's fourth leading consumer of cut flowers, following the Netherlands, Germany, and England. The United States follows Japan and Norway.

ON AN AVERAGE DAY...

... Japanese have to pay

... $3.87 for a roll of Kodak film (24 exposures)

... $9.49 for a can of tennis balls

... $11.34 for a movie ticket

... $19.76 for Revlon lipstick

... $23.00 for a pound of sirloin steak

... $70.00 for an auto-reverse Walkman

... $650 to rent one square foot of retail space on the Ginza (Tokyo's commercial district) for one year

NOTE: Surprisingly, the only item that is less expensive in Japan is an American product, Kodak film. Americans pay an average of $4.23 for Kodak film, $3.42 for a can of tennis balls, $5.25 for a movie ticket, $4.74 for Revlon lipstick, $9.00 for a pound of sirloin steak, $50.00 for a Walkman, and $550 for one square foot of retail space on New York's 57th Street.

ON AN AVERAGE DAY...

... Japanese spend $199,517,500 on food
Of that,
... $30,326,660 is spent in restaurants

NOTE: Americans spend $945,111,233 on food. Of that, $403,684,247 is spent eating out. In both Japan and the United States, the percentage of food dollars spent eating out has grown rapidly in recent years. More single parents, more dual-career couples, and less free time are all cited as reasons for this trend.

ON AN AVERAGE DAY...

... 2,021 Japanese are cremated

... 152 Japanese are buried

NOTE: Largely a result of the lack of available land in Japan, a majority of residents choose to be cremated when they die. In contrast, a majority of Americans choose to be buried, with 5,195 prefering conventional burial and 742 choosing cremation.

NOTES
AND
INDEX

SOURCE

3. *Japan Statistical Yearbook*
4. Same
5. Japan Health and Welfare Statistics Association
6. Ministry of Health and Welfare
7. *Japan Statistical Yearbook*
8. Same
9. Same
10. Same
11. *The Japan Times*
12. Japan Health and Welfare Statistics Association
13. *Japan Statistical Yearbook*
14. Same
15. *The Japan Times*
16. Same
   The Economist
17. *The Japan Times*
   The Christian Science Monitor
18. National Police Agency
19. *Japan Statistical Yearbook*
20. Japan Health and Welfare Statistics Association
21. Same
22. *Japan Statistical Yearbook*
23. National Police Agency
24. Same
25. Same
26. Same
27. *Journal of Japanese Trade & Industry*
28. Japan Health and Welfare Statistics Association
29. *Japan Quarterly*
30. *Health Affairs* (cited in *The New York Times*)
   Journal of Japanese Trade & Industry

NOTE SOURCE

3. Bureau of the Census
4. *Statistical Abstract of the United States*
5. National Center for Health Statistics
6. Same
7. Bureau of the Census
8. Same
9. *Statistical Abstracts*
10. Bureau of the Census
11. *The Japan Times*
12. *Statistical Abstract*
13. Same
14. Same
15. National Center for Health Statistics
16. Same
17. Same
18. National Center for Missing Children
19. *Statistical Abstract*
20. National Center for Health Statistics
21. Same
22. Same
23. *Statistical Abstract*
24. National Safety Council
25. National Center for Health Statistics
26. Same
27. *Journal of Japanese Trade & Industry*
28. Japan Health and Welfare Statistics Association
29. *Statistical Abstract*
    United Network for Organ Sharing
    American Medical News
30. *Health Affairs* (cited in *The New York Times*)
    Journal of Japanese Trade & Industry

SOURCE

31. *Population Bulletin*
32. Same
33. Japan Health and Welfare Statistics Association
34. *The Japan Times*
35. National Police Agency
36. *Journal of Japanese Trade & Industry*
37. Same
38. *Journal of the American Chamber of Commerce in Japan*
39. *Tobacco Reporter*
40. Same
41. *Japan Statistical Yearbook*
42. Same
43. Same
44. Same
45. The Worldwatch Institute
46. *Japan Statistical Yearbook*
47. Same
48. Same
49. The Worldwatch Institute
50. *Japan Statistical Yearbook*
51. The Worldwatch Institute
52. *Public Innovation Abroad*
53. Foreign Press Center/Japan
54. *U.S. News & World Report*
55. The Worldwatch Institute
56. *The Japan Times*
57. *The Japan Economic Journal*
58. *Look Japan*

NOTE SOURCE

31. National Center for Health Statistics
32. *Statistical Abstract*
33. Same
34. National Council for Alcoholism
35. Bureau of Justice Statistics
36. *Journal of Japanese Trade & Industry*
37. Same
38. *Journal of the American Medical Association* (JAMA)
   Bureau of the Census
39. *Tobacco Reporter*
   Forbes
40. Same
41. *Statistical Abstract*
42. Bureau of Justice Statistics
43. Same
44. U.S. Forest Service
45. The Worldwatch Institute
46. *Statistical Abstract*
47. Same
48. Same
49. The Worldwatch Institute
50. *Statistical Abstract*
51. The Worldwatch Institute
52. Motor Vehicle Manufacturers Association (MVMA)
53. American Public Transportation Association
   N.Y.C. Transit Authority
54. *U.S. News & World Report*
55. The Worldwatch Institute
56. *The Japan Times*
57. *On An Average Day . . .*
58. Same

SOURCE

59. *Public Innovation Abroad*
60. Environmental Agency Government of Japan
    Tokyo Business Today
61. The Worldwatch Institute
    Tokyo Business Today
62. *Look Japan*
63. The Environmental Investigations Agency (cited in *USA Today*)
64. *The Japan Economic Journal*
65. *The New York Times*
66. Japan External Trade Organization (JETRO)
67. Same
68. *Japan Statistical Yearbook*
69. National Police Agency
70. Same
71. Same
72. *The Economist*
73. National Police Agency
74. Same
75. Same
76. Same
77. Same
78. Same
79. Same
80. Same
81. *Japan Statistical Yearbook*
82. *Asahi Evening News*
83. *Tokyo Business Today*
84. Same
85. Same
86. *Japan Statistical Yearbook*

59. *Public Innovation Abroad*
60. *On An Average Day . . .*
61. The Worldwatch Institute
62. *New Perspectives Quarterly*
63. The Environmental Investigations Agency (cited in *USA Today*)
64. *The Economist*
65. *The New York Times*
66. Pet Food Institute
67. American Veterinary Medical Association
68. *Statistical Abstract*
69. Bureau of Justice Statistics
70. *Statistical Abstract*
71. *On An Average Day . . .*
72. Federal Bureau of Investigation (FBI)
73. *Statistical Abstract*
74. Same
75. Same
76. Same
77. Same
78. National Police Agency/Japan
79. Same
80. Same
81. *Statistical Abstract*
82. Same
83. *Journal of Japanese Trade & Industry*
86. *Statistical Abstract*

SOURCE

87. Same
88. Same
89. *Look Japan*
90. *Japan Statistical Yearbook*
91. Same
92. Amway Corporation
    The Wall Street Journal
    Nation's Business
93. *Japan Statistical Yearbook*
94. Same
95. *Japan Economic Journal*
96. *The Japan Times*
97. *Japan Statistical Yearbook*
98. Same
99. Same
100. Same
101. *The Japan Times*
102. Institute for Social Research (cited in *The New York Times*)
103. Same
104. Same
105. *The Japan Times*
106. *Japan Statistical Yearbook*
107. Same
108. Same
109. Foreign Press Center/Japan
110. *Tokyo Business Today*
111. *Japan Statistical Yearbook*
112. *Journal of Japanese Trade & Industry*
113. Electronic Industries Association of Japan

87. Same
88. Same
89. *The New York Times*
90. *Statistical Abstract*
91. Same
92. *The Wall Street Journal*
    Amway Corporation
93. *Statistical Abstract*
94. MVMA
95. *Japan Economic Journal*
96. *The Japan Times*
97. *Japan Statistical Yearbook*
98. *On An Average Day* . . .
99. *Statistical Abstract*
100. Same
101. Institute of International Education (cited in *U.S. News & World Report*)
102. Institute for Social Research (cited in *The New York Times*)
103. Same
104. Same
105. *Statistical Abstract*
106. Survey Research Center, University of Michigan
107. Same
108. Same
109. A.C. Nielsen
     Radio Advertising Bureau
110. *Statistical Abstract*
111. Motion Picture Association of America (MPAA)
112. Cable Television Advertising Bureau
113. U.S. Consumer Electronics Industry Association

SOURCE

114. *Billboard*
115. Foreign Press Center/Japan
116. Same
117. Same
118. Same
    The Washington Post
119. Foreign Press Center/Japan
120. Ministry of Posts and Telecommunications
121. Same
122. Same
123. Same
124. *Japan Statistical Yearbook*
125. *The New York Times*
126. The Worldwatch Institute
127. *The New York Times*
128. Same
129. *Statistical Abstract of the United States*
130. Same
131. JETRO Monitor
132. *The New York Times*
133. National Police Agency
134. *Worldscope* (cited in *Crain's New York Business*)
    American Banker (cited in *U.S. News & World Report*)
135. *The Wall Street Journal*
136. *Japan Statistical Yearbook*
137. Same
138. *Business JAPAN*

114. *Video Store*
     Video Marketing
115. American Newspaper Publishers Association
116. MPAA
117. Foreign Press Center/Japan
118. *The Washington Post*
119. *Statistical Abstract*
120. Same
     Business Tokyo
121. *Statistical Abstract*
     Cellular Tellecommunications Industry Association (cited in *USA Today*)
122. *Statistical Abstract*
123. AT&T
124. *Statistical Abstract*
125. *The New York Times*
126. Same
     Statistical Abstract
127. *The New York Times*
128. Same
129. *Statistical Abstract*
130. Same
131. JETRO
132. *The New York Times*
133. *Statistical Abstract*
134. *Worldscope* (cited in *Crain's New York Business*)
     American Banker (cited in *U.S. News & World Report*)
135. *The New York Times*
136. *Statistical Abstract*
137. U.S. Patent and Trademark Office
138. *Business Japan*

SOURCE

139. Council on Competitiveness (cited in *The New York Times*)
140. JETRO
141. *The New York Times*
    IDD Information Services (cited in *USA Today*)
142. The Japan Society (cited in *Fortune*)
143. *Japan Statistical Yearbook*
144. JETRO
145. *Japan Statistical Yearbook*
146. JETRO
147. Electronic Industries Association of Japan
148. Motor Vehicle Manufacturers Association (MVMA)
149. Japan Motor Business
    MVMA
150. Robotic Industries Association
151. Same
152. *USA Today*
153. *The Japan Economic Journal*
154. *The New York Times*
155. Same
156. The Worldwatch Institute
157. *The Japan Times*
158. Japan Health and Welfare Statistics Association
159. *Japan Statistical Yearbook*
160. International Savings Bank of Geneva (cited in *USA Today*)
161. *Forbes*
162. *Journal of Japanese Trade & Industry*
163. Bank of Japan
    Journal of Japanese Trade & Industry
164. JETRO
165. The Japan Vending Machine Manufacturer's Association
    (cited in *The New York Times*)

139. Council on Competitiveness (cited in *The New York Times*)
140. *Business Tokyo*
     JETRO
141. *The New York Times*
     IDD Information Services (cited in *USA Today*)
142. The Japan Society (cited in *Fortune*)
143. *Statistical Abstract*
144. Toy Manufacturers of America
145. *Japan Statistical Yearbook*
     Commerce Department
147. Electronic Industries Association of Japan
148. MVMA
149. *Japanese Motor Business*
     MVMA
150. Robotic Industries Association
151. Same
152. *USA Today*
153. *The Japan Economic Journal*
154. Business Committee for the Arts, Inc.
155. *Statistical Abstract*
156. The Worldwatch Institute
157. *Statistical Abstract*
158. American Red Cross
159. *Statistical Abstract*
160. International Savings Bank of Geneva (cited in *USA Today*)
161. *Forbes*
162. *Statistical Abstract*
163. Bank of Japan
     Statistical Abstract
164. Direct Marketing Association
165. *The New York Times*

SOURCE

166. JETRO
167. *Japan Statistical Yearbook*
168. JETRO
169. Foreign Press Center/Japan
170. U.S. Department of Agriculture
171. *The Wall Street Journal*
172. *The Japan Times*
173. *The Japan Economic Journal*
174. U.S. Department of Agriculture
175. Dentsu
    McDonald's Japan
    Business Week
176. Foreign Press Center/Japan
177. JETRO
178. Same
179. Same
180. Same
181. The Leisure Development Center/Japan
182. *Tokyo Business Today*
183. *Golf*
184. *Tokyo Business Today*
185. JETRO
186. *Japan Statistical Yearbook*
187. Same
188. Same
189. Organization for Economic Co-Operation and Development (OECD)
190. Same
191. The Leisure Development Center/Japan
192. *Amusement Business* (cited in *The New York Times*)
193. *Japan Statistical Yearbook*
194. *Focus Japan*

167. *Statistical Abstract*
168. JETRO
169. Foreign Press Center/Japan
170. U.S. Department of Agriculture
171. *Statistical Abstract*
172. *The Japan Times*
173. *The Japan Economic Journal*
174. U.S. Department of Agriculture
175. *On An Average Day . . .*
    Restaurants & Institutions
    Tokyo Business Today
176. *Journal of Japanese Trade & Industry*
    Statistical Abstract
    International Coffee Organization
177. U.S. Department of Agriculture
178. National Sporting Goods Association
179. JETRO
180. National Golf Foundation (cited in *USA Today*)
181. *Golf*
    The New York Times
182. *On An Average Day . . .*
183. *The New York Times*
185. Toy Manufacturers of America
186. MVMA
187. *Statistical Abstract*
188. Same
189. OECD
190. Same
191. *On An Average Day . . .*
192. *Amusement Business* (cited in *The New York Times*)
193. *Statistical Abstract*
194. *Focus Japan*

SOURCE

195. *Japan Statistical Yearbook*
196. The Leisure Development Center/Japan
197. *Business Japan*
    The Wall Street Journal
198. The Leisure Development Center/Japan
199. Same
200. Same
201. Recording Industry Association of America, Inc.
202. JETRO
203. Same
204. Runzheimer International
    Business Week
    Fortune
    Public Innovation Abroad
205. JETRO
206. Same

195. UNESCO
196. *The New York Times*
197. Photo Marketing Association International
    The Wall Street Journal
198. National Bowling Council
199. The Leisure Development Center/Japan
200. Same
201. Recording Industry Association of America, Inc.
202. JETRO
203. American Floral Marketing Council
204. Runzheimer International
    Business Week
    Fortune
    Public Innovation Abroad
205. *Statistical Abstract*
206. Cremation Association of North America
    Casket Manufacturers Association

INDEX

ABOUT THE AUTHOR

Thomas N. Heymann is the author of *On An Average Day . . .* , *On An Average Day In The Soviet Union . . .* , *The Unofficial U.S. Census,* and *In An Average Lifetime . . .* , all published by Fawcett Books. In addition to his work as a "people's demographer," Thomas N. Heymann is a marketing consultant and a producer of educational media. He holds a Bachelor of Science degree in Radio, Television, and Film from Northwestern University and an MBA in Marketing from Columbia University. He currently resides in Chappaqua, New York, with his wife Grace, son Gabriel, daughter Laura, and Labrador retrievers Allie and Grizzly.